Managing Your Church Finances

...Made Easy

J. David Carter

LifeWay Press
Nashville, Tennessee

© Copyright 1998 • LifeWay Press
All rights reserved

ISBN 0-7673-9442-9

Dewey Decimal Classification: 254.8
Subject Heading: CHURCH FINANCE

Printed in the United States of America

All Scripture quotations are from *The Holy Bible, New International Version*.

LifeWay Press
127 Ninth Avenue, North
Nashville, TN 37234

CONTENTS

SECTION ONE

- Introductory Material 7
- Develop a Plan and Policy 10
- Following Financial Management Procedures 11
- Basic Biblical Values and Premises 12
- How to Handle Cash Receipts 13
- Counting Committee Report Sheet 14
- Setting Up Budget Accounts 15
- Chart of Accounts 18
- How to Handle Disbursements 19
- Purchase Order 20
- How to Reconcile the Checkbook with the Bank Statement 22
- Bank Reconciliation Process 23
- How to Use a General Ledger 24
- How to Prepare Financial Statements 25
- Church Financial Statement 27
- How to Prepare and Maintain Individual Contribution Records 28
- Record of Contributions Form 29
- Procedures for Maintaining Church Members' Gifts According to Each Responsibility . . 31
- IRS Requirements for Contribution Receipts 32
- Internal Control Procedures 35
- Ten Most Common Mistakes Churches Make 36
- Employer's Quarterly Federal Tax Return (Form 941) 36
- Payroll Earning Record Form 37

SECTION TWO

- The Minister's Income and the IRS 38
- Are Ministers Self-Employed or Employees? 38
- Can the Church Withhold Taxes and Pay Them for the Ministerial Employee? 39
- How Long Should We Keep Records? 39
- Expenses, Allowances and Reimbursements 40
- Ministers' Compensation and Tax Reporting 41
- How to Handle a Housing Allowance 42
- Notification of Housing Allowance from the Church to the Minister (Sample Letter) . . . 43
- Minister's Estimate of Housing Expenses 44
- Accountable Reimbursement Plan Explained 46
- Church Staff Compensation Worksheet 48

SECTION THREE

Job Descriptions for:
    The Church Financial Secretary 49
    The Church Treasurer 50
    The Counting Committee 52
    The Church Audit Committee 54
    Church Insurance Committee 55

CONCLUSION

This manual is written in an interactive teaching style with the manual as the teacher. Each lesson has an example where applicable. It is designed to be used in a training conference or by an individual.

Thanks to several sources for materials:

- To Richard Broome (retired) and Clarence Hackett of the Florida Baptist Convention for the permission to use a similar manual as the basis for this manual
- To Publication 517 of the IRS
- To Previous writers of Job Descriptions

Section One

Church Stewardship Services Vision Statement:

We will provide leadership and resources to disciple believers in following the biblical concept of stewardship with the goal of producing spiritual renewal and revival.

Credits:

We are grateful for the generosity of the Florida Baptist Convention and its director, Clarence Hackett. They have provided valuable resources for practical application for many years. Other state leaders look to them as leaders in providing stewardship resources. Richard Broome wrote the book that gave me many of the ideas as I wrote this manual. I contacted him on several occasions for his input, and he was very gracious in helping. The Florida Baptist Convention gave us the rights to use their materials as we produced this resource. As you use these materials, give God thanks for the contribution of the leaders in Florida.

Target Audience for This Manual:

Persons who manage, plan and handle church finances.

Purpose of This Manual:

This manual is designed to help you manage your church finances. It is to be used as a training resource either in groups or individually.

Setting for Using This Manual:

This manual is a leader training resource. It is to be used in conferences to prepare church leaders to be good stewards by properly managing church financial matters. We recommend that you obtain a manual for each person who relates to church finances, such as church treasurer, stewardship committee members, financial secretary, staff members and others with similar functions.

Goals: To Train Persons to:

- Keep church financial records
- Report church financial records
- Manage individual contribution records
- Handle employee tax-related items
- Handle financial gifts
- Prepare a budget
- Determine the ministries supported by a church budget

We see several elements as key to church growth. The church's budget is a reflection of how the church membership views the Kingdom of God. The Kingdom of God is the rule of God, and as we join God in His work we enter a kingdom relationship, both individually and corporately. We come under His authority as King. As we look at the plan God has for His bride, the church, we see that the church has:

- **ONE Great Commission**
- **FIVE Functions**
    1. Evangelism
    2. Discipleship
    3. Ministry
    4. Fellowship
    5. Worship
- **FOUR Results**
    1. Spiritual Growth
    2. Numerical Growth
    3. Ministries Expansion
    4. Mission Advance

Introduction:

We are to be faithful stewards and faithful managers. The role we have as stewards of God's assets is awesome. It is amazing that God has entrusted us with such an important task. This task becomes even more focused when we see how our stewardship involves finances. We can prevent many of the problems that divide churches if we properly manage church finances. We truly *are* God's asset managers.

Your role carries much responsibility. It matters how you handle church finances, because ministries depend upon funding provided by a budget. A budget is not some sterile, number-crunching work. It is one of the most important ministries of your church. A world of unsaved persons are waiting on the funds your church provides. If they could talk to you, they would express their gratitude with smiles. "The King will reply, 'I tell you the truth, whatever you did for one of the least of these brothers of mine, you did for me" (Matt. 25:40). God is blessed by what you do for Him as you and those you lead give through the local church. Second only to giving, the responsibility of managing God's money is vital to the success of your church in fulfilling the intent of the budget. As we give, we are really giving because of our relationship to God, and as we manage, we must be acutely aware of God's plan for the church.

Have you ever evaluated why you give money through your church? Place a check mark in the box beside each reason that causes you to give.

- _____ ❏ I give because I love the Lord (Psalm 119:10).
- _____ ❏ I give because I want to be obedient (Psalm 119:34).
- _____ ❏ I give because I believe God blesses those who give, and I want His blessings (Mal. 3:10).
- _____ ❏ I give because I want to do good and not evil. I feel guilty when I don't give (Eph. 2:10).
- _____ ❏ I give because it is the right thing to do (Heb. 13:16).
- _____ ❏ I give as an act of worship (Matt. 12:42-44).
- _____ ❏ I give because I want to be a witness to those who watch my life (John 15:8).
- _____ ❏ I give in order to keep returning to the Lord (Mal. 3:7-8).
- _____ ❏ I give because my spouse considers it very important (Eph. 5:21).
- _____ ❏ I give because I honor what my parents taught me as a child (Ex. 20:12).
- _____ ❏ I give in order to win victory over my tendency toward selfishness (1 Peter 4:8-10).
- _____ ❏ I give money because it represents the priority of God in my life (Romans 11:16).
- _____ ❏ I give more than money because I seek the Kingdom (Matt. 6:33).
- _____ ❏ I give because I am not my own (1 Cor. 6:19-20).

You could have checked each of these. Now rank the answers you gave beginning with the number one reason you give. Place the number on the line beside each, in order of priority to you, and be ready to share it as a testimony. You will want to spend time reviewing your responses to determine if giving habits or motivations need to be changed.

Who in your church handles the Lord's money?
_____
_____

Actually, everyone handles the Lord's money. "The earth is the Lord's, and everything in it, the world, and all who live in it" (Ps. 24:1). "Do you not know that your body is a temple of the Holy Spirit, who is in you, whom you have received from God? You are not your own; you were bought at a price. Therefore honor God with your body" (1 Cor. 6:19-20).

Of course this question was a little "tricky" to answer, but I wanted to make a point. Some people believe that the tithe is the Lord's money but use the other 90% as if it were their own. Sadly, many Christians never come to grips with the fact that He is just as interested in how we manage the 90% as He is in our obedience in the tithe. The point is, 100% of what we have belongs to God — we have been appointed as managers of God's assets.

Persons who manage the money received for the Lord through their church should first see themselves as belonging to God. With that in their minds and hearts they will be better handlers of the Lord's money.

Develop a Plan and Policy:

A plan and policy should be in place to handle every financial issue. Those who manage finances should be trained. Several illustrations may establish the need to justify this type of training. Consider the following scenarios, and describe how you would handle each situation:

1. Suppose you are the pastor or church secretary. Someone comes by the church with the desire to give a cash amount through your church to help a family whose house burned to the ground. It is a large amount of money, and they want the right to claim it as a gift for tax reasons. They ask you to give them a letter crediting them with the gift. You want to do what is right regarding the Internal Revenue Service requirements, but the church does not have a policy or a procedure to cover that kind of gift. What would you do?

   _____
   _____
   _____
   _____

   Under the circumstances, you cannot legally accept the gift on behalf of the church nor provide the tax verification the donor needs. A person cannot give through the church to a particular person. A church can receive gifts and apply them to the situation, but the gift must come from the church. If your church does not have a line item in the budget for such purposes, then the church can give the money to the person, but cannot give the contributor verification for tax purposes unless church action is taken to create a new line item.

2. Consider that your pastor needs an additional $90.90 per month in income. Is this possible without increasing the budgeted amounts? Each of us would like to have that much more income. Suppose your church gives him $300.00 per month car allowance as part of his salary package. Is there a way for his income to increase, resulting in more spendable income, having only the information provided in this one illustration? Yes, there is a way. You will find this explained more completely in "Section Two: The Minister's Income and the IRS."

   If your budget income for the minister is currently referred to as a "salary package," consider the result of this designation. First, there is no need to establish a salary package. Second, the church may think the minister receives more money than he actually receives. A car allowance is actually a church expenditure, and not part of a minister's salary. The car allowance should be considered as accountable, reimbursable income, which is not taxable for any purpose.

   For example, remember the original stated need was for an additional $90.90 per month. Multiply $300.00 by 15.3% and put that amount in this space:_____. Now, multiply the $300.00 by 15% and add the two amounts and place that amount in this space:_____. This amount is your additional spendable money if you are in the 15% tax bracket and pay self employment taxes (SECA) or Social Security. The answers are $45.90 and $45.00 respectively, for a total of $90.90.

Establishing and following financial management procedures are important to the life of your church as we will see in the next section.

Following Financial Management Procedures

If you have not developed a church financial management procedures policy, you will find the information in this manual helpful in establishing or evaluating procedures, and you can use it to benefit your church's financial decisions. Consider these key elements in establishing proper financial procedures.

- **Authorization of Expenditures:** A church budget should be approved by the church and amended as needed. The best time for church approval is on a _____ _____. It is good to place high value on this church decision by scheduling it on Sunday morning. Amendments often increase amounts in line items to cover God's unpredictable activity. If the church votes on an amendment, it is good to use the budget adjustment as a means to report on God's activity. It is of higher value to make the report on Sunday morning. It can be a time to celebrate. For instance, if Sunday School attendance increases, defining a need to increase the literature budget, this is reason to _____. You may have completed the sentence with a word like celebrate or rejoice. As you rejoice, you will vote to increase the budgeted amount in that line item. This is a good thing. Budgets should be increased as ministry needs increase. Anytime God blesses with additional ministry opportunities, He will surely supply the needs associated with the ministry.

- **Documentation:** The church should have a plan to verify expenditures. This plan should include receipts, purchase orders, expense advances, verification of bank deposits, etc., as needed.

- **Reconciliation:** All activity in either credits or debits to the accounting system should be reconciled. A term is used in Romans 6:11 that is also used as an accounting term. The word is "reckon." This term means to balance the books. The definition is linked to another Greek word which means to take an inventory. This would be like an audit of church finances. Of course God has a way of taking an audit of our personal lives.

    Describe ways God may audit our personal finances.
    _____
    _____
    _____

- **Responsibility Assignments:** It is good to assign the individual tasks of receiving, recording, reporting, reconciling, counting, and handling financial gifts, with various persons being responsible for each of these areas. It is not a good policy for one or two person to have the responsibility for all areas.

- **Communication:** Most church members are not accountants and cannot easily read many financial statements. They just want to know basic facts about the budget. It is helpful to provide a summary, including fund balances, budgeted amounts, and summaries of receipts and disbursements. You will find an example of a summarized financial statement on page 27.

- **Qualifications:** Persons who handle church finances need to have certain qualities or qualifications. They should:
  - Possess a sense of calling from God
  - Be open and willing to receive training
  - Be capable of managing details of financial matters
  - Be persons of integrity
  - Be good stewards (Christian asset managers!)
  - Be capable of maintaining confidentiality
  - Have a good reputation
  - _____
  - _____
  - _____

- **Level of qualification needed:** The qualities listed above are more important than the professional skills of an accountant. Most persons managing God's money are volunteers. These materials are prepared for both church volunteers and employees, experienced and inexperienced. All church members need Christian values regarding money, and especially those who handle the Lord's offerings. One of the first needs is to teach biblical lessons on the way God wants us to be His stewards.

Basic Biblical Values and Premises

- God owns it all.
- We are responsible as asset managers.
- The tithe is tangible evidence that a person gives ownership to God.
- Giving and generosity involve more than finances.
- Stewardship involves the whole of life — time, talents or giftedness and possessions, including money.
- We are to seek first the Kingdom of God and His righteousness.
- _____
- _____

This section is only an introduction to these issues. You may wish to schedule a conference such as the Successful Christian Financial Management Seminar or a Stewardship Revival. You can use books, tracts, promotional materials, and other resources to provide training. For a complete list of available resources, contact Church Stewardship Services, 127 Ninth Avenue, North, Nashville, TN 37234-0182 or call 1-615-251-2808.

How to Handle Cash Receipts

1. **Use a Cash Receipt Journal:** This journal is designed to keep records of all _____ money. "Cash" includes both loose money, envelopes and loose checks. We recommend that the Counting Committee use a Report Sheet (see example on the next page). You will then post or insert the amounts directly to the General Ledger from the Report Sheets. Keep these Report Sheets in a binder for auditing purposes.

2. **Use Counting Committee Report Sheets:** You may use the example on the next page to prepare sheets for your church. Keep these in a safe place for at least two years. They are an important part of your church's financial records.

Counting Committee Report Sheet

_____ Baptist Church

Date: _____ ( ) A.M. ( ) P.M.   Deposit Number: __9-09__

	LOOSE		ENVELOPES		TOTAL
Coins:	No.	Amount	No.	Amount	Total
0.01	5	.05	7	.17	.22
0.05	5	.25	15	.75	1.00
0.10	7	.70	6	.60	1.30
0.25	6	1.50	5	1.25	2.75
0.50	4	2.00	4	2.00	4.00
1.00					
Currency:					
1.00	45	45.00	14	14.00	59.00
5.00	15	75.00	16	80.00	155.00
10.00	4	40.00	8	80.00	120.00
20.00	4	80.00	11	220.00	300.00
50.00					
100.00					
Subtotal		244.50		398.77	643.27
Checks				1,282.73	1,282.73
TOTAL		244.50		1,681.50 (1)	1,926.00 (2)

	Account No.	Debit	Credit	
Budget Offering	075		1,716.00	⎫
Literature Reimbursement	303		10.00	Entry A
Amount Deposited to Budget Bank Account (Acct. No. 001)		1,726.00 (1)		⎭
Designated Funds:				⎫
Building Fund	076		200.00	Entry B
Amount Deposited to Designated Bank Account (Acct. No. 002)		200.00 (2)		⎭

Total Offerings		1,926.00

(1) **Envelope Total** must agree with the total to be posted to individual contribution records.
(2) The total amount deposited in both bank accounts must agree with the total of the TOTAL column.

Counting Committee Signatures:

_____   _____
_____   _____

Received by Church Treasurer: _____ Date: _____

There are several ways your church receives offerings. Name as many of those ways as you can on the lines below.

_____
_____
_____
_____
_____

Basically, contributors give offerings five ways:
- By giving through the Sunday School
- By placing it in the offering plates during worship services
- By mail
- By personal delivery
- By having other persons give it on their behalf.

Some have started automatic electronic withdrawals, called 'EFT" or electronic fund transfer. Soon, persons will give to their church through the internet. Of course, there are also those who provide for their church after their death through estate plans.

Each Counting Committee Report Sheet has a two-part number on it. You actually insert the applicable number in the spaces provided. This number represents the sequence number of the offering within the month it is received. For example, Counting Committee Sheet No. 01-04 is assigned to the fourth offering in January. Therefore, Counting Sheet Report Sheet No. 09-07 is assigned to the _____ offering received in September. Each bank deposit ticket should bear the same serial number as its corresponding Counting Committee Sheet. Why would there be a 09-07 on a Counting Committee sheet when there are only 4 weeks in a month?

_____
_____
_____
_____
_____

Offerings are received more than once each Sunday. During a revival, you may have as many as seven or more offerings in one week. The Counting Committee Sheet for No. 09-07 is the seventh offering in September.

A Cash Receipt Journal contains records in two accounts. These two are:
No. 001 _____ and No. 002 _____.

Most churches have two basic accounts, the regular budget account and at least one designated account.

Account Number 001 is the account for tithes or regular budget offerings. You will not put _____ offerings in this account. Persons who give designated offerings want them going for the purpose designated. The answer is <u>designated</u> offerings. There are times when money is reimbursed to the church. Credit these funds back to the same account and line item they were taken from. See the illustration on Counting Committee Report Sheet, Account No. 303: Literature in the example on page 14.

Account Number 002 is the account for offerings given through designated accounts. You will not put _____ offerings into this account. Persons giving designated offerings want to be sure they go for the purpose they were intended. Remember tithing and giving involves people. Where people are involved, you will likely face the unexpected. What I have tried to do in this manual is to describe ways to handle church finances to prevent as many difficulties as possible. This is one reason why financial matters should be handled with integrity and sensitivity. A designated account is used for special offerings such as the building fund and special mission offerings. Add some others from your own experience:

_____   _____
_____   _____

Many churches find it is generally best to establish two bank accounts. There can be great difficulty managing these two or more distinct offerings through one bank account.

Recording receipts to the journal is illustrated on the Counting Committee Report Sheet No. 9-09 on page 14.

Budget Offering: Entry A is illustrated in both the Counting Committee Report Sheet (page 14) and the General Ledger; it is recommended to transfer the figures directly from the Counting Committee Counting Sheets to the General Ledger. The entry in the General Ledger is found as R 9-09. The letter "R" represents Cash Receipts, the number "9" represents the ninth month and 09 represents the ninth offering in September. Proper entry codes are important during audits.

Examples and Explanations: The Sunday Budget offering is $1,716.00 (page 14). Write that amount as a credit in the same line with the words Budget Offering. The church actually received additional money in the amount of $210.00. This is for two different line items in the budget — the building fund and literature. Place the $200.00 as designated money. Place $10.00 as funds reimbursed and applied back to the literature budgeted amount. Therefore, you have a grand total of $1,926.00 shown in the total offerings line.

1. An example of different accounts is found on page 18 (the Chart of Accounts). The budget is organized with numbers grouping certain primary ministries. All line items in the 100 category are for Missions. Notice as follows:

    100 = Cooperative (Missions) Ministry   400 = Music Ministry
    200 = Pastoral Ministry   500 = Administrative Ministry
    300 = Education Ministry   600 = Building and Grounds/Physical Facilities

NOTE: Additional categories can be added. This requires additional number groupings.

2. The total money received as budget receipts is $1,726.00 (page 14). That amount is added to funds available and deposited to the budget bank account. In order to show that it is deposited you will place the amount of $1,726.00 as a debit in your ledger. For accounting purposes only, the money you deposit in a bank account is considered a debit in your ledger. What will you do with the $200.00 shown as "designated" offering? Write your answer below and be ready to share it with the group.

_____
_____
_____

You will write the number $200.00 in the debit column "002" which identifies your designated bank account. You will complete a separate deposit slip, because it is going into a separate bank account from the Budget Account. Then, you will write the number $200.00 in the credit column to show that the money is in the Building Fund of the Designated Account.

CHART OF ACCOUNTS
With Trial Balance As of September 30, _____

		Debits+	Credits<->
Cash:			
1.	Cash in Bank — Budget	1,653.10	
2.	Cash in Bank — Designated	1,395.00	
Liabilities and Fund Balances:			
30	Federal Income Tax Payable		0.00
31	Social Security Tax Payable		0.00
32	Medicare Tax Payable		0.00
50	Fund Balance		1,470.10
Receipts:			
75	Receipts — Budget		58,200.00
76	Receipts — Designated		2,295.00

Disbursements:

100	**Cooperative Missions:**		
	101 Cooperative Program	5,820.00	
	102 Associational Missions	1,746.00	
	103 Partnership Missions	582.00	
	104 Community Outreach	500.00	
	105 Men's Ministry and Women's Ministry	495.00	
200	**Pastoral Ministry**		
	201 Taxable Salary	6,750.00	
	202 Housing Allowance — Pastor	1,350.00	
	203 SBC Retirement	900.00	
	204 Insurance Protection	1,332.00	
	205 Expense Reimbursement	1,382.00	
300	**Education Ministry**		
	301 Minister of Education	900.00	
	302 Housing Allowance — Min. of Ed.	900.00	
	303 Literature	900.00	
	304 Supplies and Organization Exp.	900.00	
	305 Expense Reimbursement	1,720.00	
	306 Recreation	800.00	
400	**Music Ministry**		
	401 Minister of Music	900.00	
	402 Housing Allowance — Music	900.00	
	403 Instrumentalist	900.00	
	404 Music Supplies	628.00	
	405 Expense Reimbursement	427.00	
500	**Administrative Ministry**		
	501 Secretary Salary	5,700.00	
	502 Employer's Payroll Tax Expenses	645.00	
	503 Office Supplies and Expense	1,490.00	
	504 Promotion	810.00	
600	**Building and Grounds Ministry**		
	601 Debt Retirement	8,820.00	
	602 Custodial Services	1,800.00	
	603 Utilities	2,475.00	
	604 Repairs and Maintenance	2,925.00	
	605 Supplies	985.00	
	606 Insurance	2,585.00	
	TOTALS	**$61,965.10**	**$61,965.10**

How to Handle Disbursements: Other terms for disbursements are expenses, allocations, payments, expenditures, or spending outlay. In the space below give a descriptive statement of how your church handles disbursements.

_____
_____
_____
_____

The following recommendations are very important to handle disbursements successfully.

1. Adopt a church policy for the development and adoption of the church budget.[1] Design it around ministries your church has committed to do. Certain ministries are included in all church budgets such as: missions, local pastoral ministries, benevolence, education, music, and maintenance of church property. You need to have a general policy and, in most cases, specific policies. A policy is designed to reflect the way your church chooses to handle financially-related ministries.

2. Adopt a church policy which defines the authority your church gives to those handling finances. For example, many policies have spending limits. Most churches require two or more signatures on each check. Spending above specific amounts will likely require church or committee approval. Another policy is needed for churches which provide a pastor's home, to cover things such as who will pay for repairs or replacement if a water heater goes out.

3. Adopt a policy for making purchases. It is a good policy to use purchase orders, but purchase orders might not be useful in all situations. For example, ministers can avoid paying taxes on car expenses if they are reimbursed for these expenses. It is therefore a better choice in this situation to provide them a credit or debit card to pay for gas and service charges on the car. Policies give clear definitions for the way the church has determined it will handle these matters and must apply equally to everyone. Purchase orders are used when someone needs to make a specific purchase.

---

[1] Excellent materials are available from Church Stewardship Services to help a church prepare a budget. There is specific help on how to prepare a budget with a ministry focus.

PURCHASE ORDER

No. _____

Church Name: _____

Address: _____   Phone: _____

Date of Request: _____
Date Needed: _____
Suggested Payee/Vendor: _____
              Address: _____
                        _____

Description: Acct. No.   Amount

ESTIMATED AMOUNT OF PURCHASE REQUEST $ _____

Requested by: _____   ____/____/____
Approved by: _____   ____/____/____

RECORD OF PAYMENT:

Documentation Audited By: _____   ____/____/____
Funds Verified By: _____   ____/____/____
Payment Authorized By: _____   ____/____/____

Amount Authorized for Payment: $ _____

Date Payment Due:	Date Paid:	Check No:

---

1. The church should vote to authorize those persons who will sign checks. There should be at least two signatures required. The check needs to be made out completely before both persons sign each check. No one should ever be asked or agree to sign a blank check. A checkbook should be used that provides a check stub. Complete the check stub with an account number for each check for proper accounting. Use a check protector or postage meter if available.

2. Use a filing system, with files for paid and unpaid bills. Be sure to keep receipts for each paid bill. As each bill is paid, record the date the check is mailed, the check number, and

the amount paid. Reconcile or balance the monthly bank statements. Compare each canceled check with the ledger record and check stub.

Checks, Check Stubs, and the General Ledger — Include the following information on both the check and check stub.
- To whom it is payable
- Date
- Purpose
- Amount
- Applicable budget account number

Handling a General Ledger: The General Ledger is used for both budgeted and designated accounting records.

Describe in your own words how Jesus balanced the books for us when He died on the Cross.
_____
_____
_____
_____

Balance your church financial records with the monthly bank statement. You may have a computer software program which helps you do this. If your church has a computer and financial software, what software do you use and how do you use it? Write the name of the software in the following space and place a checkmark before each thing you practice.

Our church uses _____ software. This software:

❏ Prints our checks.
❏ Records payments in the proper account by using the account name and number.
❏ Calculates the monthly report for the church in the form of a financial report.
❏ Maintains contribution records.
❏ Processes payments and receipts weekly.
❏ Processes payments and receipts monthly.
❏ Processes payments and receipts periodically.
❏ Has a password for authorized users only.
❏ Maintains a record of hand-written checks.
❏ Is backed-up each time we update our files.

How to Reconcile the Checkbook with the Bank Statement

(This is a step by step approach to reconciling a bank statement.)

1. **Step One** — Sort the canceled checks and deposit tickets in numerical order. Your church may have a bank or credit union that does not return canceled checks, but they should provide a listing of each check date and amount. You may also have a carbon copy of each check you write.

2. **Step Two** — Balance your checkbook with your ledger. If your bank does not provide canceled checks, the same information is on the monthly bank statement. Locate the check number and amount on the bank statement. Refer to your checkbook and ledger to see where you have it recorded. Place a check mark beside each check on the bank statement and also beside each place in the ledger and check stub that corresponds to the particular check. Continue this until all are verified.

3. **Step Three** — Use a Bank Reconciliation form to list each outstanding check (example on page 23). An outstanding check is one that is not yet recorded by the bank on the bank statement. The payee may have already cashed the check, but it did not arrive at the bank in time to be included on the most recent bank statement.

4. **Step Four** — Record other charges and credits. Your church may have a bank account which pays interest. The interest amount will appear on the bank statement. Record it in your ledger as a credit to the income account and as a debit to the bank balance account. You need an account number to maintain these credits. If your bank charges you a monthly fee to maintain the account, it will also appear on the monthly statement. Record it as a debit in your ledger with an account number for that particular expense item and as a credit to the bank balance account.

5. **Step Five** — Show any amounts in savings or CDs as a credit on the regular monthly financial statement. Your church probably has a savings account or certificates of deposit. These amounts should be credited back to the proper account and reported to the church on the monthly financial statement.

BANK RECONCILIATION

Statement Date: September 30, _____

Name of Bank: <u>No Rust or Moths Eternal Bank</u>

1. Balance Per Bank Statement, End of Month . . . . $<u>2,803.72</u>

2. Add: Deposits in Transit:[2]

No.	Amount
9-09	1,726.00

$1,726.00

Subtotal . . . . $ <u>4,529.72</u>

3. Subtract: Checks Outstanding (from list below) . . . . $<u>2,876.62</u>

4. Balance Per General Ledger and Running Checkbook Balance . . . . $<u>1,653.10</u>

LIST OF CHECKS OUTSTANDING:

No.	Amount	No.	Amount	No.	Amount	No.	Amount
1145	25.42						
1148	50.00						
1151	400.00						
1152	275.44						
1153	111.00						
1154	980.00						
1155	376.76						
1156	658.00						

Notes:_____

_____

Signature:_____

Reconciliation Date: _____

---

[2] Deposits in transit are made after the closing date of the latest bank statement.

How to Use a General Ledger

A General Ledger is a record of the financial history of your church. This is true whether it is in the form of a book or a computer software program. The ledger contains financial information according to account title or number. The Chart of Accounts on page 18 illustrates the Trial Balance. The Trial Balance is a listing of totals from each general account page. Each page in the General Ledger is designated for one budgeted item. This Chart of Accounts is a report of what is recorded in the General Ledger. The debit and credit columns should always be equal if the General Ledger is in balance. A Trial Balance is used as a method of establishing that the books are balanced.

The General Ledger is a double-entry system, which means that it includes a record of both debits and credits. *Debits* is the term to describe money that we have spent and the remainder (money) left in the bank for future expenditures. This is the money that is already applied to the budget. A credit is the term for money received. You will place the number that represents all budget receipts in the credit column of your ledger. If any contributions are designated for a certain budgeted item, the number representing that budgeted item needs to be credited with the designated amount.

Complete the following statement: The money you record that is moved from the credit column as a receipt and applied to the line item as taxes is called a _____. It is a debit from your budget to a line item. There are "unspendable funds" in accounts considered liabilities, such as money set aside to pay withholding tax payments. On page 18, the Chart of Accounts shows the balance in Liabilities and Fund Balance line item 50 in the credit column, as $1,470.10. This amount is included with the Cash in Bank number 1 — Budget in the amount of $1,653.10. Now subtract the $1,470.10 from $1,653.10 and what do you get? _____. This figure is $183.00, which is the amount in excess of expenditures to this date in this church year. The General Ledger provides information for current reporting and future reference. Keep the General Ledger in a fire-proof safe place indefinitely.

You can have a credit or debit balance and not have the money in the bank. The reason for this is that if your credits exceed your debits, you have overdrawn the bank account. The bank account normally has a debit balance, and the budget income account normally has a credit balance.

As you manage a church accounting system, remember that you are one of God's asset managers. Essentially, that is the role of a steward. Your role is to manage the system according to the vote of your church. It is important that you do not become so attached to this job that you allow the success or failure of the church budget to cause you to become defensive, overly protective, or possessive. God will take care of His church and His money!

Describe some of the problems you have seen in persons who had the responsibility of serving as church treasurer.

_____
_____
_____

How to Prepare Financial Statements

Church financial statements have one primary purpose, and that is to give the church a picture of the financial condition of the church. You can show the financial condition in the form of a snapshot rather than in the form of an album. Most church members only want to see the snapshot that gives them the bottom line information.

As you prepare a financial statement, summarize the ways finances have contributed to the church's ministries. In the space below, describe each area of ministry, according to the budget category (see page 18):

100 Cooperative Missions _____
_____
_____

200 Pastoral Ministry _____
_____
_____

300 Education Ministry _____
_____
_____

400 Music Ministry _____
_____
_____

500 Administrative Ministry _____
_____
_____

600 Building and Grounds Ministry _____
_____
_____

Keep the focus on *ministries* and not money. The money is a means to an end and is not the end. All line items in a budget are missions. Many apply to local missions, and many others apply to missions in the larger picture. The minister's salary is as much mission as the support of international missionaries. Yet, there is a principle God honors when we provide sacrificially for missionaries. This principle comes from unselfishness and is seen as generosity. As a result, giving is used to touch lives of those that we personally cannot ever know. International missions involves putting several values into practice such as trust, love, generosity, unselfishness, and an expanding world view.

Many church financial statements are presented as a maze of numbers without a clear picture of the financial condition of the church or its ministries. I have prepared an example of a Church Financial Statement that is the snapshot and not the album. First, let's examine the parts on a summarized financial statement. See the parts on page 27.

- **Fund Balances:** This is the summary of the month's transactions according to individual bank accounts, with the beginning and ending balances. This summary answers certain questions. How much money did we have? How much money do we have now?

- **Giving Analysis:** This analysis compares the actual money received to the planned or anticipated receipts. This is calculated, based upon the year-to-date amount and the most recent month.

- **Summary of Income and Disbursements:** The money is spent, and the balance budgeted for each category is stated. This means that you know the amount budgeted for cooperative ministry, the amount spent, and the remaining balance.

- **Debt Deductions:** Another term for debt is *liability*. It is good to show the interest, principal, and balance of all debts. You may show the length of time remaining on the debt if payments are made as scheduled, and also include the rate of interest on the loan.

- **Bills Unpaid:** This lets the church know that there are outstanding bills yet to be paid. Include the due date for the unpaid bills. It is best to let the church know the status of these bills on a regular basis.

- **Budget Disbursements:** This shows the total amount spent for each budgeted item. Some budgeted items, such as property insurance, may be payable yearly. This means that you may have eleven months of budget without expenditures. Then, there is a sudden large expenditure. This can be your experience with several line items, such as lawn maintenance, summer camps and Vacation Bible School.

- **Information to Include:** Page one of the financial statement is the page for the summary report. You can provide more detailed information on additional pages. It is good to distribute these reports at all weekly services (Sunday mornings as well as Wednesday evenings). You can also include a summary report when you mail the quarterly individual financial statements. The purpose of a financial statement is to have an informed congregation. Note the example of a Church Financial Statement on the facing page.

CHURCH FINANCIAL STATEMENT

Fund Balances:

Account	Balance __/__/__	Receipts	Transfers	Disbursements	Balance 9/30/__
Budget Account	1,738.10	6,580.00	(100.00)	6,565.00	1,653.10
Special Account - Building	1,095.00	200.00	100.00	0.00	1,395.00
Totals	2,833.10	6,780.00	0.00	6,565.00	3,048.10

Giving Analysis:

Monthly Budget Receipt Requirement	1,538.46
September Receipts (4 Weeks)	1,645.00
Total Receipts Year-to-Date	58,200.00
Average 39 Sunday Receipts	1,492.31

Summary Budget Receipts and Disbursement:

	September	Monthly Budget	Nine Months	Nine Months Budget
Receipts	6,580.00	6,667.00	58,200.00	60,000.00
Disbursements:				
100 Cooperative Ministry	1,030.00	1,034.00	9,143.00	9,300.00
200 Pastoral Ministry	1,359.00	1,400.00	11,714.00	12,600.00
300 Education Ministry	730.00	733.00	6,070.00	6,600.00
400 Music Ministry	400.00	425.00	3,755.00	3,825.00
500 Administrative Ministry	943.00	967.00	8,645.00	8,700.00
600 Building and Grounds Ministry	2,103.00	2,108.00	19,590.00	18,975.00
TOTAL	6,565.00	6,667.00	58,917.00	60,000.00

Mortgage Payable to: No Rust or Moths Eternal Bank, Inc.

	Balance 9-1-__	Interest	Principal	Balance 9-30-__
	70,900.00			
September Payment:	980.00	440.00	540.00	70,360.10

SCHEDULE OF BILLS UNPAID, SEPTEMBER 30, _____

Payable to:

	Acct. No.	Amount
A - Painting Contractors	604	500.00

How to Prepare and Maintain Individual Contribution Records

Individual records represent a history of each person's financial stewardship. A giving record often represents struggle, trust, faith, obedience, sacrifice and much more. This is a record of regular budget offerings and special offerings. An example of an individual contribution record is shown on the next page.

Contact LifeWay Envelope Service for information on the various offering envelope systems that are available. LifeWay Envelope Service can help you determine the best envelope system for your church. Call 1-800-874-6319 (or send FAX to 615-251-5603), and give them Code CSS-98 to receive special pricing. *(Sample Envelopes Below)*

AN OFFERING ENVELOPE SYSTEM THAT PRODUCES RESULTS:

Monthly Mailing

A regular, in-home reminder of your stewardship program can have dramatic results for your ministry.

With our Mailing Program, customized offering envelopes are sent directly to your members' homes on a regular basis — **monthly, bimonthly or quarterly**.

MAKES SENSE — reminds your members frequently of their contribution commitment.

Boxed Sets

Adult Stewardship Message Series
Features predetermined weekly Bible messages — printed in a beautiful full color design.

Children's Boxed Sets
Choose from our Bible Trivia envelopes each printed with a Bible trivia question and answer to stimulate learning or our Children's Stewardship sets — one that is right for every age. Both encourage giving and are designed to promote a positive use of time and talents.

Custom Message Series
You choose the messages that will be printed on your Custom Boxed Set envelopes. This provides weekly opportunities to inspire and motivate your members.

Personalized Boxed Sets:
Enjoy all the benefits of Custom Boxed Sets with a "personal touch." These are printed with your members' names and addresses and mailed directly to their homes.

Envelope No.	**RECORD OF CONTRIBUTIONS**
	Church Finance Record System

NO GOODS OR SERVICES WERE PROVIDED OTHER THAN ANY "INTANGIBLE RELIGIOUS BENEFIT" FOR ANY OF THE CONTRIBUTIONS REPORTED ON THIS STATEMENT.

Your church appreciates your tithes and offerings. Please compare with your records and report any errors.

Name:

Address:

Phone:

Year Beginning

Budget Pledge
$_____ Per Week

Sunday	First Quarter	Second Quarter	Third Quarter	Fourth Quarter	Date	Special Gifts	Amount
1						Memorial	Amount
2						Building	
3						Revival	
4						Missions	
5							
1							
2							
3							
4							
5							
1							
2							
3							
4							
5							
Received This Quarter							
Received to Date							
					Total Special for Year		
					Total Budget for Year		
					Total Budget and Special for Year		

It is important to keep good records and to send quarterly thank-you notes with the individual contribution records. An example of a quarterly thank-you note might be:

Your quarterly and year-to-date gifts to the work of God have helped our church receive $_____ *(Insert the amount that is true for your church.)* This amount is used for ministries that are larger than what any of us can do alone. On behalf of all these ministries, thank you. A copy of the church financial statement is enclosed for your review. You will also find a copy of your contribution record. Please check it to be sure the amounts are correct. If they are not correct, please contact the financial secretary. Again, thank you very much for your commitment and faithfulness to God's work.

The purpose of doing this is to:
- Be accountable to those who give to the church's ministries
- Encourage those who give
- Place value on their gifts and commitment
- Call attention to the corporate success through synergy
- Supply them a copy of their individual giving records for review
- Provide them a copy of the church's latest financial report

Confidentiality is essential in recording and reporting individual records. Church counting committees should be composed of persons who keep confidences. Access to individual contribution records should be held to those who, of necessity, must work with the receipts. This policy of limited access should be communicated to the church. There are exceptions, such as when a church elects deacons and requires that they be tithers. Someone needs to access this information for verification purposes. Under these circumstances, it is necessary to provide this confidential information to the appropriate deacon qualification committee.

Persons keeping these records include volunteers as well as financial secretaries. These persons should be elected whenever other church officers are elected. It is good to rotate persons through this position to avoid pitfalls. But, remember to be gentle when trying to change a system that has been in place for some time, and be sensitive to the feelings of all those involved.

Procedures for Maintaining Church Members' Gifts According to Each Responsibility:

1. The Counting Committee will:
   - Arrange the envelopes numerically or alphabetically. If you keep records by number, then they will arrange them by number. Otherwise, arrange them alphabetically. Checks without envelopes should be arranged alphabetically, for ease in posting to contribution records.
   - Total all gifts by using an adding machine with a tape for records. Attach this tape to the Counting Committee Report Sheet, and have the counter sign the tape.
   - Loose change is counted as such, and the amount is written on the Counting Committee Report Sheet as illustrated on page 14.

2. The Church Financial Secretary or Church Treasurer will:
   - Record each gift to the applicable church member's individual contribution record. Double-check each envelope to verify that the check has been removed. This takes a little extra time. You will sometimes find money not found by the counting committee.
   - Record the amount of the gift in the appropriate space according to the date. Some offering envelopes allow space to give to more than one item using one check. Some contributors may put more than one check in one envelope. Use the following space to explain why someone may do that.

   _____
   _____
   _____

   - Put the envelopes and copies of each form completed in a storage box to be kept for three years. You can easily store this information on a computer disk. You keep these records to support church members who may be audited by the IRS or when a church member needs access to church giving records.
   - Maintain records on a weekly basis.
   - Record special gifts and total them at the end of the year, not necessarily by quarter.
   - Mail the quarterly individual contribution records. You may want to save money by not mailing these, but in the long run, it will cost you. Church members like to receive their quarterly thank-you notes. Some review their giving plans and notice they have to catch-up on missed giving, or they may see errors that require correction before tax time.
   - Mail the records before the second Sunday of the next quarter. Your fiscal year may be different from the following example, but it will illustrate the way to do it. For our purposes, consider the fiscal year as the calendar year. This means that you mail the first quarter's individual contribution records before the second Sunday of April and continuing.

   When would you mail the second quarter?_____
   Third quarter? _____
   Fourth quarter? _____

- Mail the yearly report before the end of January of the new year. This means that there will be four mailings per year. Many wait for their third quarter record before making year-end contributions. The yearly report contains the last quarter's record as well as the year-to-date records. Some mail a fifth mailing during the middle of December to encourage end of the year contributions. If you follow this plan, use it to promote the special Christmas Lottie Moon Mission Offering.
- Maintain individual contribution records for a minimum of four years. This four-year minimum is based on IRS audit guidelines.

IRS Requirements for Contribution Receipts

Church giving records are not very important to most church members until they receive an audit notice from the Internal Revenue Service. Suddenly, they need verification for what they claimed to give, and this verification must come from their church. Some have even asked church leaders to falsify the documents to keep them out of trouble. In these cases, they have stolen from God by not tithing. Then, they have tried to steal from the government by claiming deductions for which there was no gift. This is a very serious matter, both for the individual and the church. At least two experienced and mature Christian leaders should review this matter with the person being audited. Church records need to be properly maintained in order to be ready when persons need access to their records.

Your church can be a good steward of receipts as you follow a good plan. Effective January 1, 1994, any single gift of $250.00 or more to a church, or other charity, can be deducted on the donor's Federal Income Tax Return only if a written receipt has been received by the donor prior to the filing of the return. Canceled checks, or receipts which show insufficient information or only summary totals, are no longer acceptable by the IRS for such gifts.

Receipts must show the following information:
- Name and address of the church
- Name of the contributor
- Date and the amount of each single gift of $250.00 or more. You already do that if you keep financial records according to the regular contributions.
- Date and description of any non-cash gift valued by the contributor at $250.00 or more. Your church does not have to validate the value of this type gift. It is the responsibility of the contributor to get an appraisal to determine the value of the gift.

Persons may want to claim as contributions money paid to the church for tuition, weddings, receptions, personal counseling, field trips, holy land trips, and other like-kind services which is unlawful. This has caused IRS to require value statements of anything received in exchange for any goods, money, or services given in exchange for goods and services. These are not legitimate contributions. If the church gives a contribution receipt, it must show that the allowable amount credited to the contributor is in excess of the value of whatever the contributor received in exchange for the contribution.

As an example, John and Susan have a son who went on a church trip that cost $250.00 per child. They prayed and decided to pay (into a scholarship fund established by the church) enough to cover expenses for any two others who could not pay their own way. Their check was for $750.00. They are credited for the amount over the benefits they obtained for their own son, or $500.00. The church gives them a contribution credit for $500.00. Gifts like this are called "quid pro quo" by IRS. If they do this, the church must explain what that one check was used for. The explanation may look something like this:

Total Check:	$750.00
Payment for Son's Trip:	-250.00
Gift for any 2 Youth Trips:	$500.00

Following is an example of another type of gift which must be handled in a special manner:

Suppose a generous person found a bargain on a TV/Video at an appliance store and bought it for the church. She has a receipt to verify the cost. Most often, this person would like to have some acknowledgment. Write her a thank-you letter, but do not put the value of the TV/Video in the letter. Write something like this:

Thank you for your gift. Please keep this receipt for your records and claim this on your tax return. According to IRS, the church cannot name an amount and add it to your contribution record. Therefore, your contribution record will not show this gift, but you can claim it, using your receipt for verification. There is a line on the IRS form for non-cash contributions. Write the amount you can prove to IRS in that space.

Add the following statement to the acknowledgment letter:

NO GOODS OR SERVICES WERE PROVIDED OTHER THAN ANY "INTANGIBLE RELIGIOUS BENEFIT" FOR ANY OF THE CONTRIBUTIONS REPORTED ON THIS STATEMENT.

The following example form provides the information needed by each contributor at the end of each year.

Cash Contribution Statement		
Church		
Church Address		Zip
To: Place the name and address of the contributor in this space.	Date: _____	

The following is a list of cash contributions made by you and received by the church on the dates shown. Please compare your records with this listing, and notify the financial secretary within 90 days if you have questions concerning any amount listed or not listed. After 90 days, statements not questioned will be assumed to be accurate, and supporting documentation, such as offering envelopes, may be discarded. ANY GOODS OR SERVICES PROVIDED TO YOU OR YOUR FAMILY BY THE CHURCH IN CONNECTION WITH ANY GIFT LISTED ON THIS STATEMENT WERE OF TOKEN VALUE ONLY OR CONSISTED ENTIRELY OF AN INTANGIBLE RELIGIOUS BENEFIT.

Date Received	Purpose	Amount

Total This Column: _____

This form is for cash contributions only.

Date	Purpose Received	Amount

Total This Column: _____
Total Both Columns: _____

Computer software programs are available that will maintain this up-to-date information as someone records the information each week. If your church does not have a computer and wants to gain access to this kind of record system, there are businesses which provide an accounting service. There is a charge, but it may even be less expensive to use one of these services. Many accountants provide this service for a very reasonable fee.

Churches which have never provided contribution records must at least issue a receipt for each gift of $250.00 or more. This receipt must show the contributor's name, the date and amount of each single gift of $250.00 or more. Include a statement similar to that which appears on the example shown in capitalized letters on the previous page.

If any goods or services were provided in exchange for any contribution of $75.00 or more, disclosure of the details and value of the goods or services must appear on the contribution statement or receipt for that gift instead of the statement concerning "intangible religious benefits only." The church or charity must inform the contributor in writing of the amount (which is limited to the amount by which the gift exceeds the value of the goods and services) that can be claimed as a contribution. No disclosure is required if the goods or services were of token value only. *Token Value* is defined in the IRS regulation as a value (a good faith estimate of actual value when documented value is not available) which does not exceed the lesser of $64.00 or 2% of the contribution.

Internal Control Procedures

Internal Control is a plan to protect assets, verify accuracy, and encourage efficiency for maintenance of church financial records. The following suggestions are born out of experience and wisdom. It is good to include these in a policy.

- Assign different persons the tasks of counting the offering, writing the checks, recording individual contributions, and reconciling the bank statement.

- Schedule counting and depositing times and processes, and faithfully follow them with trained persons designated to handle these functions.

- Require two signatures on each check. No more than one signer should be a paid staff member. Enlist people (to sign checks) who know and understand the budget and who will question anything unusual or irregular.

- Maintain an inventory of church assets.

- Secure a bond from your insurance company to cover each person handling money.

- Assign two persons to deposit the offering in the bank or place it in a night deposit.

- Promptly deposit all money.

- Encourage each church and Sunday School member to use an individual offering envelope.

- Make payments after supporting documentation has been approved by an authorized person.

- Conduct an annual audit.

- Develop and maintain a procedure for each facet of handling money.

Ten Most Common Mistakes Churches Make

- Improperly classifying employees as self-employed (independent contractors)
- Failing to furnish a Form W-2 to each employee (including ministers) and/or a Form 1099-Misc to certain non-employees
- Failing to include taxable fringe benefits (such as non-accountable expense reimbursements, social security supplements, and "special occasion" gifts) in wages on Forms W-2
- Including the minister's housing allowance in wages on Form W-2
- Failing to offer church employees available nontaxable fringe benefits
- Failing to provide church employees with an accountable expense reimbursement plan
- Including in the ministers "pay package" the budgetary cap for an accountable reimbursement plan
- Providing contribution receipts to members who donate their services to the church
- Providing contribution receipts for donations designated to other individuals without proper organizational control
- Failure by churches that operate, supervise, or control a private school to timely file an annual Certificate of Racial Nondiscrimination (Form 5578)

Employer's Quarterly Federal Tax Return (Form 941)

Churches with employees other than ordained ministers must file a Form 941 each quarter, by April 30, July 31, October 31, and January 31. Ordained ministers must file their own personal quarterly estimated tax returns. The church is exempt unless it has another type employee. You may find detailed instructions by obtaining Circular E, Employer's Tax Guide, which is mailed to each employer with Form 941.

I have included an example of a completed Form 941. The items correspond to items used elsewhere in this manual.

FORM 941 EXAMPLE:

Line 2	Total wages subject to withholding, plus other compensation	5,650.02
	Write the total of all taxable salaries paid — (do not include Housing Allowance on this line)	
Line 3	Total income tax withheld	702.00
Line 4	Adjusted total of income tax withheld	0.00
Line 5	Adjustment of withheld income tax	702.00
Line 6a	Taxable Social Security Wages (2,800.02 x 12.4%)	347.20
	Write the total of taxable salaries paid to NON-ORDAINED STAFF ONLY on this line.	
Line 7	Taxable Medicare Wages (2,800.02 x 2.9%)	81.20
	Write the total of taxable salaries paid to NON-ORDAINED STAFF ONLY on this line.	
Line 8	Adjustment of social security and medicare tax	0.00
Line 10	Adjusted total of social security and medicare tax	428.40
Line 14	Total taxes	1,130.40
Line 17	Total deposits for quarter	1,130.40
Line 18	Balance Due	0.00

NOTE: Be sure to carefully follow IRS instructions for depositing taxes during the quarter. Many churches will be able to send one check payable to Internal Revenue Service with Form 941 at the end of each quarter.

The following is a record of payments with dates and specific amounts. Maintain this record in a separate place from the church financial statement. This is a record of the quarterly taxes paid for each employee.

Payroll Earning Record — Quarter Ending September 30, (year)

S. S. No	Name	Notes	Taxable Salary	Housing Allowance	Fed. Income Tax	S.S. Tax	Medicare Tax	Net
123-45-9999	Pastor	(1)	2,250.00	750.00	600.00	0.00	0.00	2,400.00
234-56-8888	Minister of Education	(2)	300.00	300.00	0.00	0.00	0.00	600.00
345-57-7777	Minister of Music	(2)	300.00	300.00	0.00	0.00	0.00	600.00
456-78-9999	Organist	(3)	300.00	0.00	0.00	18.80	4.38	277.02
567-89-5555	Financial Secretary	(4)	1,900.02	0.00	102.00	117.78	27.54	1,652.70
678-90-4444	Custodian	(3)	600.00	0.00	0.00	37.20	8.70	554.10
	TOTALS		5,650.02	1,350.00	702.00	173.58	40.62	6,083.82

(1) Ordained Minister — housing allowance designated in advance; written voluntary agreement with the church to withhold Federal Income Tax
(2) Ordained Ministers — both part-time; housing allowance designated in advance; no agreement to withhold Federal Income Tax
(3) Part-time employees — not minister; not independent contractors per IRS 20 Criteria
(4) Full-time employee — not ordained and not classified as a minister

Section Two

The Minister's Income and the IRS

The time you spend in properly preparing church records can save your pastor and staff from difficult situations. IRS Publication 517 is entitled *Social Security and Other Information for Members of the Clergy and Religious Workers*. Churches are exempt from Federal Income Tax, Federal Unemployment Tax, and even the filing of a Form 990 Information Return. Yet churches are not exempt from reporting salaries and wages paid or the withholding of any required Federal Income Tax, Federal Insurance Contributions Act (SECA) or Social Security and Medicare Taxes on amounts paid to non-ordained employees. The ordained employees normally pay quarterly returns, and the church is not responsible for reporting this income. A church may make a one-time election not to withhold and match SECA and Medicare Tax on amounts paid to non-ordained staff.

Are Ministers Self-Employed or Employees?

A minister's earnings for the services he performs are subject to self-employment tax unless he has requested an exemption. To obtain an exemption for self-employment tax, a minister must meet all of the following conditions:

- Be conscientiously opposed to public insurance because of his individual religious considerations (not because of general conscience), or be opposed because of the principles of his religious denomination.
- Establish that the organization is a church or a convention or association of churches. File for other than economic reasons.
- Inform your church that you are opposed to public insurance.
- Establish that the organization that ordained him is a tax-exempt religious organization.
- Complete Form 4361 by the date his income tax return is due and he has net earnings as a minister of at least $400.00 in the year of his return.
- Sign the form the IRS mails to him after he receives the Form 4361.

Is it good to file an exemption? This is an important decision. By doing this, a minister will lose Social Security benefits paid previous to the two years before he filed Form 4361. There are additional rules in Publication 517.

An ordained minister is considered a self-employed person for social security tax purposes, but he is considered an employee for income and retirement plan tax purposes. Some of his income may be considered income from self-employment while other income may be considered income from wages.

Common-Law Employee: Under "common-law" rules, a minister is considered an employee or a self-employed person depending on all the facts and circumstances. Generally, he is an employee if your employer has the legal right to control both what he does and how he does it, even if he has considerable discretion and freedom of action. Obtain a copy of Publication 15-A. If he is employed by a congregation for a salary, he is generally considered a common-law employee, and income from the exercise of his ministry is considered income from wages for income tax purposes. However, amounts received directly from members of the congregation, such as fees for performing marriages, funerals, or other personal services, are considered income from self-employment.

If any of the following is true, the minister is considered an employee for income tax purposes. Does the minister provide:

- Instructions
- Training
- Integration
- Personal Service
- Hiring, Supervising, and Paying Assistants
- A Continuing Relationship with Set Hours
- Full-time Work on Premises, Set Work Order Reports
- Pay by the Hour, Week, or Month
- Business and Travel Expenses
- Tools and Materials
- Investment
- Profit or Loss
- Work for More Than One Company at a Time
- Serving the Public
- Have the Right to Fire
- Have the Right to Quit

Can the church withhold taxes and pay them for the ministerial employee?

Ordained persons performing the services of a minister are exempt from the withholding requirements of the law; however, your church can enter into a voluntary agreement with the ordained ministers to withhold and pay Federal Income Taxes on their behalf. No other taxes can ever be withheld from the minister's wages. It may be best to establish a bank account where the minister can have an amount equal to all the taxes automatically deposited on his behalf. Then, the minister can access that money to pay the quarterly estimated tax payment. Essentially, this is a savings plan. Use IRS Publication 15, Circular E, Employer's Tax Guide to determine the amount of income taxes to withhold.

Churches that file Form 8274 for exemption from FICA, SECA and Medicare Tax must withhold and pay Federal Income Tax for non-ordained employees. At the end of each year, and before the last day of January of the new year, your church needs to provide to employees, guest speakers, and any other contract worker, the appropriate forms.

Form W-2 — Ordained Ministers
1099 — Contract Worker, such as Guest Speaker

How Long Should We Keep Records? File and keep individual payroll earning records indefinitely. Keep the church's copy of IRS forms at least four years.

Expenses, Allowances and Reimbursements

It is highly possible that you can increase the minister's take-home money without having to increase his present salary. To do so, use an "accountable reimbursement plan." In actuality, the take-home money can be increased with proper salary designations and tax benefits. Tax allowance is designed to give the taxpayer the maximum benefits when taking the legal tax benefits.[3]

The best way to provide maximum benefits is to provide an accountable reimbursement plan for business expenses. The requirements are quite simple.

1. The expense much be directly related to church business.

2. There must be a reliable record.

3. The salary should not be a "package plan" which often includes car allowance, business lunches, books, additional costs such as convention, continuing education, and church-related entertainment. Each of these business expenses can be included in one line item in a church budget, designated "Church Business Expenses." In order to validate these business expenses, the minister will submit a receipt or car mileage record for each item claimed as a business expense. If he has to go out of town to be with a church member for surgery and stay overnight in a hotel, the costs of travel, hotel, and food expenses are considered business expenses. He will keep receipts for each of these and submit them for accountable reimbursement. These expenditures are church business expense and not salary or personal expense. This money is taken from the church budget account designated Church Business Expense. The receipt must show the amount, date, and business purpose before reimbursement is made.

4. Timely reporting is required as follows:
   - Expenses must be reported within 60 days.
   - Any advance in excess of the allowable expenses must be returned within 120 days.

5. This expense reimbursement cannot be made by salary reduction or by including the amount as part of a salary package. Following is a sample reimbursement policy.

---

[3] See facing page for a more complete explanation of the accountable reimbursement plan.

Sample Reimbursement Policy

In accordance with income tax regulations 1.162-17 and 1.274-5 (e), the _____ Baptist Church hereby establishes a reimbursement policy for all ministers and staff members with the following terms and conditions:

1. The church will reimburse only ministry-related expenses incurred by a minister or staff member. Reimbursement is subject to budget limitations. Such expenses will include:

   - Business use of an automobile
   - Business travel away from home including auto or air travel, lodging and meals
   - Convention and conference registration and travel expenses
   - Educational expenses
   - Subscriptions, books, tapes and other church-related educational materials
   - Entertainment and hospitality expenses in connection with church business.

2. The minister or staff member will account for each allowable expense in writing at least monthly. Documentation will include the amount, time, place, and business purpose of each expense. A receipt will accompany the documentation.

3. The minister or staff member will return advances or reimbursements that exceed actual business expenses.

4. Under this accountable arrangement, the church will not report amounts reimbursed as taxable income on the minister's or staff member's Form W-2. The minister or staff member will not report reimbursed amounts as income on Form 1040 for personal income tax purposes.

Ministers Compensation and Tax Reporting

A minister is classified as self-employed for Social Security (SECA) and Medicare purposes and as an employee for Income Tax purposes. This is a unique classification. These two different classifications can be both good and bad. They are good if the minister and the church properly handle the way salary, housing, and business expenses are listed in the church budget or according to a church policy.

Applicable statements regarding the treatment of ministers as self-employed:

- Ministers pay self-employment taxes at 12.4% for Social Security up to a certain amount that changes year to year. There is an additional amount called Medicare Taxes which applies to the total salary amount at a 2.9% rate.

- Ministers get benefits from a housing allowance if the money is designated and used for housing. This allowance must be a line-item in the budget. The minister reports this for Social Security purposes but not for income tax purposes.

- The minister who lives in a church-owned home will report as income the fair market rental value which is applicable to Social Security and Medicare taxes only.
- Additionally, a housing allowance can be provided by the church. This allowance includes furniture, cleaning supplies, lawn equipment, household items, and any other items that would apply if he owned his own home.
- In most cases, ministers can claim the cost for interest on a mortgage as a tax deduction for income tax purposes.

Applicable statements regarding the treatment of ministers as employees:

- Under this definition, ministers do not include housing allowances as taxable income. In fact, it is not reported on Form W-2. As the church financial person totals the salary of a minister, the amount designated for housing allowance is omitted.
- The intent is to reduce the taxable amount to the lowest level as you take advantage of each tax benefit. If possible, develop a church budget to give all the benefits to the pastor.

Consider the following example. The pastor has a salary package of $50,000.00 per year including $400.00 per month for car allowance. This $400.00 per month is considered compensation and will be taxed at whatever tax rate he is in. If he is in the 15% rate, then $60.00 per month would be paid in income tax, 12.4% for Social Security, and 2.9% for Medicare insurance, which is $61.20, for a total tax cost of $121.20. Of course, he can deduct his expenses off his taxable income, but he will only receive a percentage of the amount to reduce his taxable income.

Ordained ministers are exempt from the withholding requirements of the law on ministerial earnings. No taxes can be withheld legally unless there is a written voluntary agreement between the church and its minister for income tax withholding. Many ministers are motivated to be sure to have the estimated taxes saved each quarter to be available when they are due. A good way to handle this is for the pastor to open a savings account at the same bank the church uses. He will figure the amount needed each quarter and make regular deposits in order to have the money when it is due. Additionally, he will earn a small interest on the deposits. This account should only be used for this purpose. All ordained ministers qualify for this provision.

How to Handle a Housing Allowance

Housing allowance must be designated in advance by the employing church. Sometime before the end of the current year, each minister should submit to the church an estimate of housing costs for the next year. See the suggested form on page 44.

Notification of Housing Allowance
from the Church to the Minister

_____(Date)_____

Dear _____,

This is to advise you of actions taken at the business meeting of _____*(Name of Church)*_____ Baptist Church held ___*(Month)*___, _*(Day)*_, _*(Year)*_. Accordingly, $ _____ of the total payments to you during the year _____, and each year thereafter, will constitute housing allowance, unless and until the amount for future payments is changed by church action.

You must keep an accurate record of your home-related expenditures to substantiate any amounts excluded from your income in filing your federal income tax return. You are responsible for reporting to IRS as "Other Income" any amount received as housing allowance in excess of the amount actually spent to provide housing. Also, you are responsible for including your housing allowance in the calculation of any self-employment tax liability. If a parsonage is provided, add the fair market value of housing.

Under Section 107 of the Internal Revenue Code, an ordained minister of the Gospel is allowed to exclude from gross income the housing allowance paid as part of the compensation to the extent used to provide a home. If the church provides a parsonage, the fair market value can be excluded in the same manner.

This action is recorded in the church minutes.

Sincerely,

_____
(Signature, Title)

Minister's Estimate of Housing Expenses

To:_____ From:_____
                (Church)   *(Minister)*

Subject: Housing Allowance for ___*(Year)*___

The amounts below are an estimate of the payments I expect to make during ___*(Year)*___ to provide a home.

ITEM	AMOUNT
• Payments on purchase of house including down-payment, mortgage principal payments, interest, taxes or rent of leased premises.	_____
• Garage Rental (if not included above)	_____
• Utilities	_____
• Insurance	_____
• Repairs and Maintenance	_____
• Purchase of furnishings	_____
• Other housing expenses	_____
• _____	_____
• _____	_____
TOTAL:	$_____

Date:_____ _____
                                                              (Minister's Signature)

- The church or authorized committee must designate the amount of the housing allowance. A minister who owns his own home can use annual salary increases to apply that amount to the principal balance on the loan and increase the housing allowance each year.
- This housing allowance designation should be in writing.
- This designation can never be retroactive.
- To determine the maximum amount the minister can claim as housing allowance, calculate the following options and choose the lowest of the three:
    1. The amount designated by the church in advance as rental, utility or housing allowance.
    2. The actual expenses of the minister for providing the home.
    3. The fair rental value of the home, furnishings, and utilities.
- It is the minister's responsibility, and not the church's responsibility, to report the housing allowance. The church will not include the housing allowance on the minister's W-2 form.
    1. The minister is required to report on Line 22 of Form 1040 any other income related to housing allowance which exceeds what was actually used for housing. For instance, the housing allowance was $7,000.00 and the minister used $6,500.00. The additional $500.00 will be entered on Line 22 of Form 1040.
    2. The minister will also report the housing allowance on Form 1040SE, including the amount of Social Security and Medicare taxes required, based upon the amount of the housing allowance.

The minister's income may, and usually does, include remuneration which is not included as a budgeted item by the church. This additional income includes pay or income from ministerial services, such as bonuses, love offerings, Christmas gifts, retirement gifts, the value of personal use of employer's automobile, and honoraria.

- Housing allowance is not taxable for income tax purposes, according to law.
- If your church does not use an accountable reimbursement plan, all car allowances, and other allowances that are part of a salary package, must be reported as taxable earnings.
- Fringe-benefit insurance for ministers and other employees should not be included as taxable income. However, such payments are most always taxable income for persons who receive Form 1099.

Non-taxable fringe benefits:
- Parsonage or housing allowance (ministers only)
- Group Term Life Insurance Premiums for $50,000 or less of face value of insurance
- Medical Insurance premiums
- Tax-sheltered annuities — IRC Sect. 403(b), the retirement plan for Southern Baptist churches
- Accountable reimbursement plan

- A cafeteria benefit plan includes most non-taxable fringe benefits. You can choose from the menu, such as: dependent care, day care, medical deductibles, medical co-payment, eye glasses and contact lenses, and prescription medication. This type of benefit program is complicated for many churches. It may be best to find someone who specializes in this business to set up a cafeteria plan for your church. Unless your church has 25 or more employees, it is generally best to use the medical savings account which covers medical costs.

- Medical savings accounts — This type of account applies to medical expenses. This plan requires a high deductible, with the lowest annual deductible at $1,500.00 for one person and $3,000.00 for a family. The Annuity Board does not offer high-deductible insurance. Each person should seek qualified assistance when making a determination about medical coverage.

Accountable Reimbursement Plan Explained

You will not want your minister to pay unnecessary taxes. The accountable reimbursement plan has been mentioned earlier, and we will now consider more detail, including the advantages and disadvantages. There is also information on how to set up one of these accounts for your church. The minister can deduct certain expenses under this plan, but the issue is whether or not he gets the tax benefit from the deductions.

Advantages of the accountable reimbursement plan:

1. Avoids including the amounts that are reimbursed as "church business expenses" as salary to the minister. Doing so may create the impression that he makes more than he actually makes in net income.

2. Avoids the possibility that the employee will be unable to deduct expenses because of the standard deduction. The standard deduction increases each year. Because the standard deduction is so high, the minister with a pastorium may lose the car allowance if he does not use an accountable reimbursement plan.

3. Avoids the reduction for Schedule A, "miscellaneous expenses" caused by the 2% of adjusted gross income (AGI) floor. This works as follows: Include all itemized deductions, total them and reduce them by 2%. The percentage that you reduce medical itemized deductions is by 7.5%

4. Avoids the expense reduction caused by the Deason (court case) expense allocation rule. Avoids the statutory 50% reduction for meals and entertainment expenses.

    Illustration: If the housing allowance is $250.00 per month of a total salary of $1000.00 per month and the minister wishes to deduct business use of the telephone, books, car, entertainment and et cetera, he may only deduct 75% of these expenses, because his housing allowance is 25% of his total salary. In the Deason case, the judge ruled that the portion of taxable earnings cannot be reduced by the amount of the expenses that related to non-taxable earnings. By using the accountable reimbursement plan, you will avoid this issue.

Disadvantages of the accountable reimbursement plan:

1. Employees must keep detailed expense records.
2. The reimbursement plan cannot be considered as a part of an employee's salary package.
3. The budgeted amount is not payable unless the expense amount is actually used and paid after proper receipts are presented. The church can allow a per-mile amount for automobile expenses. The minister must verify whatever is claimed.
4. The person writing the checks must have full authority to deny reimbursement of those items that are not properly validated.

One of the church's primary business expenses is an automobile. It is not unusual for a minister to put in excess of 25,000 miles per year on a car. The church can credit the minister any amount for reimbursement of the use of an automobile, even though IRS allows 32.5[4] cents per mile. If a minister uses an automobile as little as 18,000 miles per year for church business and the church reimburses according to the IRS rate, he would receive $487.50 per month. This money is not taxable for any purpose if the church uses the Accountable Reimbursement Plan. Otherwise, the minister can pay as much as $_____ for Social Security and Medicare tax, and a minimum of $_____ in income tax.

To compute the tax due, use 15.3% for Social Security and Medicare and 15% for income tax. Neither the minister nor the church will want ministers to pay unnecessary taxes. The accountable reimbursement plan is a way to save large amounts of money, through proper handling by the church.

---

[4] This is the allowable amount for 1998. Check IRS publications for allowable amounts in previous or subsequent years.

Church Staff Compensation Worksheet

NOTE: Churches should be aware of recent changes in tax laws that impact how they handle paying ministers. It is better for a church to pay benefits and ministry-related costs than to give the minister a salary package.

Budget Year: _____
Today's Date: _____

Name:_____ Position:_____

Date of Employment:_____ Base Salary:_____

1. EMPLOYER-PAID FAMILY PROTECTION BENEFITS (Paid directly to Provider)
    - Annuity Board Church Plan (10% of compensation) $_____
    - Insurance $_____
    - Disability Insurance $_____
    - Medical Insurance $_____

    OPTIONAL BENEFITS:
    Housing Equity Fund (Taxable as Income) $_____
    Social Security Tax Offset (Taxable as Income) $_____
                                              TOTAL $_____

2. CHURCH MINISTRY EXPENSES PAID BY REIMBURSEMENT
    (Minister must account to the church with records.)
    - Auto Expense $_____
    - Continuing Education (Books, Journals, Courses) $_____
    - Training Conferences (Related to Church Ministries) $_____
    - Hospitality Expense (Related to Church Ministries) $_____
    - Convention Expense $_____
                                              TOTAL $_____

3. MINISTER'S SALARY (Take Home Pay)
    - Base Salary $_____
    - Cash Housing and Utilities Allowance $_____
                                              TOTAL $_____

4. SALARY ADJUSTMENTS TO BE CONSIDERED
    - Estimated Cost of Living Adjustment $_____
    - Merit Raise Increase $_____
                                              TOTAL $_____

Section Three
Job Descriptions

The Church Financial Secretary

The Church Financial Secretary is often elected annually; however, it is helpful if the same person maintains responsibility for this task. Should this office be filled with a church member or a non-member? List one reason why it should and one reason why it should not be filled by a church member.

Should _____
_____

Should Not _____
_____

Qualifications — A Financial Secretary should:
- Be Trustworthy
- Be willing to be held accountable
- Possess accounting skills
- Possess computer skills, if required
- Be Available

Option: Some churches contract with an accounting service. Then the responsibilities of the Financial Secretary would be assigned to this accounting service. Contracting with an accounting service does not negate the need for the Counting Committee, the Audit Committee, or the Church Treasurer.

Responsibilities:

1. Arrange church offering envelopes by number or alphabetically. This will automatically arrange families together, for ease in recording contributions.
2. Arrange all special offering envelopes and miscellaneous receipts alphabetically.
3. Record amounts from all envelopes and miscellaneous receipts in the correct spaces on the individual contribution records. Use an additional sheet for visitors. Label this sheet "Visitors."
4. Box, date, and store all offering envelopes and miscellaneous records of receipts. Keep them until the first quarter of the next year, at a minimum. Some churches keep these as long as they keep the contribution records listed below (minimum of three years).
5. At the end of each quarter, total all individual contribution records and mail them to the contributors. Keep the church's permanent contribution records for a minimum of three years.
6. Total special gifts at the end of each year.

The Church Treasurer

The church treasurer is an officer of the church. The character of this person should model the highest Christian lifestyle. List in the spaces below character traits you expect in the life of a church treasurer.

- _____
- _____
- _____
- _____
- _____
- _____

The church treasurer holds a position that can give confidence to the entire budget process. This person's life needs to be a model of a Christian steward. If the church treasurer is not honest with God in regard to giving God first place in his or her finances, it will be difficult for this person to call other Christians to be good stewards.

The church treasurer is elected by the church upon recommendation of the church nominating committee. He is generally elected for a term of one year, although your church may consider this position for a three-year term.

In smaller-size churches the treasurer often performs some or all of these functions:

- Church Treasurer
- Financial Secretary
- Business Administrator
- Disbursing Officer
- Stewardship Committee chairperson
- Counting Committee Member
- Audit Committee Member

The church treasurer works according to church policy, procedures, and guidelines. The Accounting Section of the Stewardship Committee recommends changes and additions to existing policies and procedures. If the church does not operate with an Accounting Section of the Stewardship Committee, the church treasurer makes recommendations as needed.

The church treasurer holds a sacred trust in handling God's money entrusted to him or her by the church. There are four primary areas of work where the church treasurer functions: receiving, recording, disbursing, and reporting. The treasurer is responsible for these functions even though he or she may delegate the tasks. Following is a suggested system.

1. **The Treasurer Receiving**

    A. Gifts received during worship services and Sunday School
    (1) After the gifts are received and counted by the Counting Committee, deposits are immediately made in the bank night depository with a duplicate deposit slip given to the church treasurer.

(2) The church treasurer verifies the deposit with the bank the next business day by telephone, fax or in person.

B. Other Gifts Received

(1) As gifts are received, other than at worship services or Sunday School, they are credited to the purpose as given, recorded to the contributor's record of contributions and deposited in the bank with a copy of the deposit slip given to the church treasurer.

(2) The church treasurer handles resources given by wills and trusts in cooperation with the Financing Section of the Stewardship Committee. These resources are reported to the church as receipts are recorded. Such funds are often designated to a certain use; therefore, monthly status reports should be given to the church. It may be best to enlist an Estate Section of the Stewardship Committee to handle endowments and like-kind funds. If there is a decision to be made as to the use of estate funds, it should be a church decision (true of undesignated gifts or bequests).

C. At the end of each month, the church treasurer reports to the church all gifts received and how they are allocated. This report is coordinated with the stewardship committee. Earlier in this manual you will find suggestions on how to clearly give financial reports to your church.

2. The Treasurer Recording

A. A church financial record system is selected by the Accounting Section of the Church Stewardship Committee and submitted to the church for approval. Your church has likely already made this decision.

B. The treasurer recommends to the church any needed changes in the accounting system. Many churches are using computers, which may present the need for church action. Examples of the new computer-generated reports should be provided and explained during report times for several months in order to help educate the people to understand them.

C. The treasurer is responsible for recording all receipts and disbursement of church funds.

3. The Treasurer Disbursing

A. The church treasurer acts on the authority of the church for disbursing of funds. The treasurer does not have the authority to pay non-budget items without instructions from the church.

B. Insufficient funds to pay bills often presents an emergency situation. Such situations require the action of the Budget Section of the Stewardship Committee or the Finance Committee if there is no stewardship committee, as church policies and procedures dictate. Your church can vote to allow a limited action to be taken in times of emergency. Otherwise, it is best to bring the matter before the church. Sometimes the emergency can be handled by announcing the need in a worship service. Some churches give this authority to a church business manager.

C. Cooperative Program, Associational Missions, and other percentage offerings are frequently tied to the budget receipts and should be disbursed as you make other payments.

D. Disbursement should be made by check with the necessary signatures. It is best to use two persons to sign each check. The church may wish to designate an alternate signer to cover for a regular, authorized check signer who may not be available.

4. The Treasurer Reporting

A. An informed church is more interested and active than an uninformed church. Therefore, the reporting should be both interesting and clear. On page 27 in this manual you can find an example of a Church Financial Statement that summarizes the financial situation of the church.

B. The church treasurer is responsible for giving a monthly financial report to the Stewardship Committee who, in turn, reports to the church.

The Church Treasurer and other persons who handle church money should be bonded. The church's insurance company possibly can add this to the existing insurance, protecting your church. There is a special insurance section on page 55.

The Church Counting Committee

The Church Counting Committee is elected by the church upon recommendation of either the Committee on Committees or the Nominating Committee. The number required for this committee is at least three. If your church is large enough, it is appropriate to enlist several persons who can rotate from week to week fulfilling these responsibilities. This is one of the committees that provides proper internal controls on the way the offerings are managed. To maintain proper checks and balances, the Financial Secretary, Church Treasurer, and disbursing officer should never serve on this committee.

Responsibilities:

- Count worship service and Sunday School offerings
- Prepare and sign deposit slips
- Prepare a Counting Committee Report Sheet (see page 14 for an example)
- Mark and organize offering envelopes numerically or alphabetically (or the Financial Secretary, see page 49)
- Make deposits in the night depository at the bank

Development of These Responsibilities:

1. **The Sunday School Offerings** — Two members of the Counting Committee should go to the Sunday School Secretary's office near the end of the Sunday School time, pick up the sealed envelopes containing the Sunday School offerings, and place them on the altar. If you have multiple Sunday Schools, it may be best to take the money to the bank for overnight deposit. Then, at least three persons from the Counting Committee would go to the bank on Monday to count the money. If the money is placed on the

altar, the Committee must stay with the offering until the worship service begins. Some churches may choose to handle these offerings in another manner.

2. **Worship Service Offerings** — Allow gifts to remain in the offering plates in the sanctuary until the end of the worship service. At least two members of the Counting Committee will be seated near the front of the sanctuary during the worship service. They will pick up the offering immediately following the service and take it to the Counting Committee room where it is counted using the following procedure.
   - Separate loose offering from the envelope offerings.
   - Count the loose offering and record the amount on the Counting Committee Report Sheet and the bank deposit slip.
   - Separate budget offering envelopes from any special offering envelopes. If the church uses the multiple purpose offering envelope, record the way the offerings are designated.
   - Open each envelope and remove the money, being sure to remove all of it.
   - Verify the amount enclosed with the amount on the face of the envelope. If there is a discrepancy or if the figures are not legible, record the amount in red on the right hand upper corner of the envelope.
   - Total the budget offering envelopes and record the amount on the Counting Committee Report Sheet and the bank deposit slip.
   - Add special offering envelopes and record the total.
   - Prepare an envelope for each loose check so that you will have a record of this contribution information.
   - Organize the cash according to the size of the bill; count each stack, and record the total on the Counting Committee Report Sheet and the bank deposit sheet.
   - Sign or initial the Report Sheet and the bank deposit sheet.

3. **Envelope Arrangement**
   - Arrange church offering envelopes in numerical or alphabetical order.
   - Arrange all special offering envelopes/miscellaneous offering receipts alphabetically.

4. **Depositing**
   - After counting the money, make three copies of each record (see page 14).
   - Take all offerings to the bank and deposit them in the night depository. At least two Counting Committee members should take them to the bank.
   - Provide the duplicates or copies of the signed deposit slip and the completed Counting Committee Report Sheet to the treasurer and financial secretary.
   - Follow this same procedure for all church services.
   - Never take offerings home!
   - Never place the offering in a safe at the church. There are several reasons not to, and one reason is enough to make the point clear. Several persons usually know the combination to the safe. If for any reason, the recorded totals are not correct, each of these persons could be blamed, even though no one had done anything wrong. The incorrect total could be only a counting or recording error.

5. **Bonding** — Every member of the Counting Committee should be bonded for personal and church protection. The insurance company is usually able to provide coverage for this committee without the members being named.

The Church Audit Committee

An audit is an examination of the church financial records in order to verify the handling, disbursing, accounting and reporting of church receipts.

The Church Audit Committee is elected annually by the church and should be composed of at least three members. Persons serving on this committee are not to serve on the Church Counting Committee, nor should they be involved in receiving or disbursing church funds. This committee handles the annual audit of the church budget. Most often, this committee enlists a third party, such as a Certified Public Accountant, to audit the church books.

This committee has a two-fold purpose.

1. To provide the church with assurance that all funds have been handled according to the will of the church, expressed through its policies and procedures.
2. To provide an appraisal of the effectiveness with which the accounting responsibilities are performed.

Responsibilities of the Church Audit Committee

1. Spot-check the offering envelopes to verify the individual record of contributions.
2. Verify bank deposit slips with the entry in the financial records.
3. Spot-check disbursements for proper entry and distribution of charges to various budget accounts.
4. Check the accuracy of the total in all accounts.
5. Determine if approved procedures have been followed in the handling of church funds.
6. Study the insurance program of the church to determine if sufficient amounts are carried. If the church has assigned someone else this responsibility, such as the Properties Committee, the Audit Committee would not perform this task.
7. Study the retirement and employee insurance programs to determine if adequate protection is provided. If another committee such as a Personnel Committee has been assigned this responsibility, the Audit Committee would not perform this task.

The Church Audit Committee should annually submit a list of church members who are to be bonded, including but not limited to:

- Church Treasurer
- The Counting Committee
- The Sunday School General Secretary
- The Church Financial Secretary
- The Church Secretary
- Others who handle church funds.

The Church Audit Committee should report all findings to the Church Stewardship Committee and the church administrator. The Stewardship Committee Chairperson will make a report to the church. If the church does not have a Stewardship Committee, the Audit Committee will give the report directly to the church.

Church Insurance Committee

We live in a rapidly changing world. Church insurance is such an important matter that it should be evaluated annually. There is far more to church insurance than fire insurance to cover buildings. Use the following evaluation to examine your church's insurance policies.

Insurance is as much a necessity for a church as it is for your home, if not more so. Church leadership has an obligation to provide for the security and well-being of the congregation; consequently, they must provide sufficient insurance.

In the spaces below, name the different types of insurance that your church needs. Then, read each insurance topic and determine if your church is adequately covered.

1. _____
2. _____
3. _____
4. _____
5. _____
6. _____
7. _____
8. _____
9. _____
10. _____
11. _____
12. _____
13. _____
14. _____
15. _____
16. _____

❏ **Building and Contents**
This coverage should include fire, extended coverage to include lightning, windstorm, hail, explosion, smoke and water damage, riots, vehicle damage, burglary and theft, vandalism and malicious mischief. Your church can maintain a savings account to self-insure for part of the coverage and to allow a high deductible, which reduces the cost of insurance. Consider both "all risk" and replacement-cost coverage. Replacement cost means that replacement of damaged property is provided at current cost even though the damaged property may have been purchased a long time before. Your insurance provider often charges a small additional fee for replacement coverage, but it is generally worth the cost. Coverage for specific items, such as computers, may require an insurance rider.

❏ **Additional Expense Coverage**
This applies to the necessary extra expenses incurred to continue operations as nearly normal as possible following damage to the building or its contents by an insured peril.

❏ **Specific "All Risk" Coverage**
This is insurance to cover items such as stained glass windows, silver, brass, objects of art, musical instruments, and other like-kind property.

❏ **Burglary and Theft Insurance**
This insurance applies to money and securities, both on and away from the premises, and other property on and off premises, such as theft of sound equipment used when the church is ministering off-site.

- **Fidelity Bonds**

  No one wants to believe that any church-going person would ever be untrustworthy, but bonds are designed to protect the individual as well as the church. A blanket position bond provides coverage on church positions rather than on individuals. This coverage should be endorsed extending the definition of employee to include uncompensated officers, trustees, and volunteers who handle church funds. Everyone who handles church funds should be bonded.

- **Boiler and Machinery Insurance**

  This coverage should be written to provide replacement cost. This is essential if there are steam boilers, since basic property insurance excludes damage resulting from the explosion of steam-pressure vessels. Also, under most state laws, most boilers are required to have periodic inspections and certification. This service is usually offered automatically by the boiler inspectors for the insurance company. Insurance can also be provided for damage resulting from an accident to the air-conditioning equipment and other types of electrical equipment and machinery.

- **Public Liability Insurance**

  This insurance covers the premises and all operations incidental thereto against bodily injury or property damage. Be certain that this coverage applies to any day school, bazaar, or other fund raising activity, meetings, picnics, sports activities, or other church-related activities conducted either on or off the church property. This insurance should include Products Liability Insurance and an eleemosynary endorsement requiring the permission of the church before the insurance company can use, as ground for defense in any law suit, any immunity that the church might otherwise have.

  Recognition should be given to the church's potential catastrophe hazard and the liability limits should be sufficient to protect against multiple claims that could arise from a single occurrence, such as an explosion or falling roof.

- **Medical Payments Insurance**

  This is a form of coverage which covers all reasonable medical, surgical, and dental expenses and applies to congregation members as well as guests. The ability to quickly pay a medical expense regardless of fault can prevent costly and embarrassing litigation.

- **Professional Liability Endorsement**

  This coverage protects the church and the ministerial staff from claims arising from counseling activities. This covers the minister and church when someone may sue, claiming they have been given bad advice.

- **Earthquake Insurance**

  This insurance can be added by endorsement to the basic property insurance policy.

- **Flood Insurance**

  Your church may obtain this insurance from your insurance company or through the National Flood Insurance Program. State geological maps show areas most likely to have a flood. If your church has a mortgage, the mortgage company may require this insurance.

❏ **Automobile Insurance**

Liability insurance should be provided on all church-owned, borrowed, leased or otherwise used under church sponsored conditions. This includes claims made arising from employees or others using their own personal automobiles on church business. Include automatic medical payments coverage, plus comprehensive and collision insurance coverage as needed on church-owned automobiles, vans or buses.

❏ **Workmen's Compensation Insurance**

This insurance provides for injuries a church employee may experience while performing duties related to his or her job.

❏ **Group Accident Insurance**

This insurance is designed to protect churches against accidents involving day school students or participants in the church's activities, such as youth day trips or senior adult travel.

❏ **Ministers and Employee Protection Program**

Every church is a steward of its ministerial leadership and has a stewardship responsibility for all of its employees. The ministers and employees protection program should include:

- A retirement program with the Annuity Board, SBC (which provides retirement based on 10% of the total compensation of the ministers and employees of the church) contributed annually, should be the minimum for every church.
- Life, medical, and disability coverage should be provided, not only as protection for the ministers and employees, but as a protection for the church.

Some churches may consider many of these coverages unnecessary, and indeed, some may not apply to all churches. It is, however, important to review the church insurance plans periodically to make sure any changes in church programming are adequately covered.

At least once a year, church leadership, preferably the Accounting Section of the Church Stewardship Committee, should review all insurance policies with the insurance company representative. Both the ministerial staff and the lay leadership are involved in providing proper protection of church property and persons on the premises. Every church should enlist the most capable church members to review and recommend, on an on-going basis, the church insurance plan.

CHRISTIAN GROWTH STUDY PLAN
Preparing Christians to Serve

In the **Christian Growth Study Plan (formerly Church Study Course),** this book *Managing Your Church Finances . . . Made Easy* is a resource for course credit in **the Stewardship** Leadership Diploma Plan. To receive credit, read the book, complete the learning activities, show your work to your pastor, a staff member or church leader, then complete the following information. The form may be duplicated. Send the completed page to:

Christian Growth Study Plan
127 Ninth Avenue, North, MSN 117
Nashville, TN 37234-0117
FAX: (615)251-5067

For information about the Christian Growth Study Plan, refer to the current Christian Growth Study Plan Catalog. Your church office may have a copy. If not, request a free copy from the Christian Growth Study Plan office (615/251-2525).

MANAGING YOUR CHURCH FINANCES . . . *MADE EASY*
COURSE NUMBER: LS-0174

PARTICIPANT INFORMATION

- Social Security Number (USA Only)
- Personal CGSP Number*
- Date of Birth (Mo., Day, Yr.)
- Name (First, MI, Last) ❏Mr. ❏Miss ❏Mrs. ❏
- Home Phone
- Address (Street, Route, or P.O. Box)
- City, State, or Province
- Zip/Postal Code

CHURCH INFORMATION

- Church Name
- Address (Street, Route, or P.O. Box)
- City, State, or Province
- Zip/Postal Code

CHANGE REQUEST ONLY

- ❏Former Name
- ❏Former Address — City, State, or Province — Zip/Postal Code
- ❏Former Church — City, State, or Province — Zip/Postal Code
- Signature of Pastor, Conference Leader, or Other Church Leader
- Date

*New participants are requested but not required to give SS# and date of birth. Existing participants, please give CGSP# when using SS# for the first time. Thereafter, only one ID# is required. *Mail To:* Christian Growth Study Plan, 127 Ninth Ave., North, MSN 117, Nashville, TN 37234-0117. Fax: (615)251-5067